SandCastle™

Baby
African Animals

It's a Baby Wildebeest!

Kelly Doudna

Consulting Editor, Diane Craig, M.A./Reading Specialist

ABDO
Publishing Company

Published by ABDO Publishing Company, 8000 West 78th Street, Edina, Minnesota 55439.

Copyright © 2009 by Abdo Consulting Group, Inc. International copyrights reserved in all countries.

No part of this book may be reproduced in any form without written permission from the publisher. SandCastle™ is a trademark and logo of ABDO Publishing Company.

Printed in the United States.

Editor: Liz Salzmann
Content Developer: Nancy Tuminelly
Cover and Interior Design and Production: Mighty Media
Photo Credits: Ablestock, Digital Vision, iStockPhoto (David T. Gomez, Jose Quintana), Peter Arnold Inc. (Michel & Christine Denis-Huot, Fritz Polking, A. Rouse), ShutterStock

Library of Congress Cataloging-in-Publication Data

Doudna, Kelly, 1963-
  It's a baby wildebeest! / Kelly Doudna.
    p. cm. -- (Baby African animals)
  ISBN 978-1-60453-159-6
1. Gnus--Infancy--Juvenile literature. I. Title.

QL737.U53D687 2009
599.64'59139--dc22
                          2008015361

SandCastle™ Level: Transitional

SandCastle™ books are created by a team of professional educators, reading specialists, and content developers around five essential components—phonemic awareness, phonics, vocabulary, text comprehension, and fluency—to assist young readers as they develop reading skills and strategies and increase their general knowledge. All books are written, reviewed, and leveled for guided reading, early reading intervention, and Accelerated Reader® programs for use in shared, guided, and independent reading and writing activities to support a balanced approach to literacy instruction. The SandCastle™ series has four levels that correspond to early literacy development. The levels are provided to help teachers and parents select appropriate books for young readers.

Emerging Readers
(no flags)

Beginning Readers
(1 flag)

Transitional Readers
(2 flags)

Fluent Readers
(3 flags)

SandCastle™ would like to hear from you. Please send us your comments and suggestions.
sandcastle@abdopublishing.com

Vital Statistics

for the Wildebeest

BABY NAME
calf

NUMBER IN LITTER
1

WEIGHT AT BIRTH
25 to 35 pounds

AGE OF INDEPENDENCE
1 year

ADULT WEIGHT
300 to 600 pounds

LIFE EXPECTANCY
20 years

About one-half million wildebeest calves are born each year. They are all born within a three-week period.

The births usually happen in January, February, or March.

Mother wildebeests
give birth in the middle
of the herd.

Wildebeest calves can stand and run three to seven minutes after they are born.

A wildebeest calf is active more quickly than any other mammal baby.

Calves nurse until they are four to nine months old.

Wildebeests are herbivores. They eat short grasses on the plains and in open woodlands.

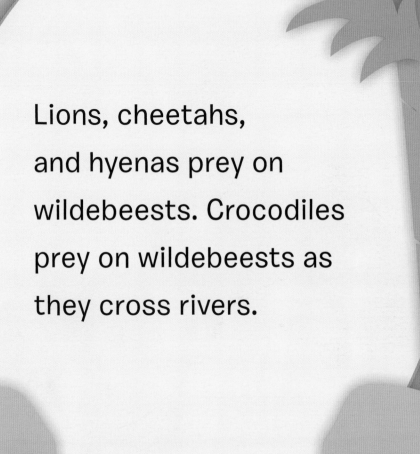

Lions, cheetahs, and hyenas prey on wildebeests. Crocodiles prey on wildebeests as they cross rivers.

Gnu is another name for wildebeest. This name sounds like a noise the wildebeests make.

Wildebeests also snort loudly and moan.

More than one million wildebeests move to areas with greener grass every May or June. This is the largest migration of any animal.

Calves stay with their mothers until new calves are born. Then the older calves leave their family group.

Fun Fact

About the Wildebeest

The whole herd of wildebeests drinks 660,430 gallons of water each day. That's enough to fill five Olympic-sized swimming pools!

Glossary

birth – the moment when a person or animal is born.

expectancy – an expected or likely amount.

herbivore – an animal that eats mainly plants.

herd – a group of animals that are all one kind.

independence – no longer needing others to care for or support you.

mammal – a warm-blooded animal that has hair and whose females produce milk to feed the young.

migrate – to move from one area to another, usually at about the same time each year.

nurse – to feed a baby milk from the breast.

plain – a large, flat area of treeless land.

prey – to hunt or catch an animal for food.

snort – to make a short, loud noise by breathing out suddenly through the nose.

woodland – an area that has trees.

To see a complete list of SandCastle™ books and other nonfiction titles from ABDO Publishing Company, visit **www.abdopublishing.com**.

8000 West 78th Street, Edina, MN 55439

800-800-1312 • 952-831-1632 fax